LETTERS AT WORK
A Communication Pocket Guide

Alan Barker

The Industrial Society

First published in 1993 by
The Industrial Society
Robert Hyde House
48 Bryanston Square
London W1H 2EA
Telephone 0870 400 1000

© The Industrial Society 1993
Reprinted 1995, 1997, 1998, 1999, 2001

ISBN 085290 996 9

Reference 1595tw5.01

British Library Cataloguing-in-Publication Data.
A catalogue record for this book is available from the
British Library.

Typeset by: The Midlands Book Typesetting Company, Loughborough
Printed by: Optichrome
Cover design: Pylon

Text illustrations: Sophie Grillet

Contents

Letters Matter

Letters do not come cheap. Add the costs of stationery, postage, handling, filing time and equipment, storage space and the salaries of writer and typist: the total cost of a business letter comes out at anything over £15.

It can be cheaper to use the phone. It may even be cheaper to travel and deal with matters personally.

Millions of letters are written every day. The total cost to business is immense. We all have a responsibility to see that every letter does its job as effectively, and efficiently, as possible.

Why write letters?

A letter is personal. It expresses a relationship: between friends, colleagues, professional acquaintances, or total strangers. The nature of the relationship dictates the nature of the letter.

In the words of the advertisement, a letter shows that we care. We are seeking to *influence* the reader. The more impersonal the letter, the less effective it will be.

Letters are ambassadors for us and for our organization. We cannot go with them: they must act on our behalf. In writing a letter, we want to be seen as approachable, caring, and positive; we want our organization to be seen as friendly, efficient, and professional.

CHECKLIST: Advantages of letters

- Personal: targets an individual
- Permanent and legal record
- Has the authority of the written word
- Has a structure which displays the shape of our thoughts
- Gives the writer time to prepare
- Can be read at the reader's leisure – uninterrupted
- Commits one side or the other to action
- Promotes me/organization: professional image
- Shows that you care about the relationship
- Diplomatic: not face to face
- Can be cheaper than telephone (lengthy explanations, long distance)

The personal touch

Letters are no longer a natural form of communication. In the past, whole novels could realistically be written as a series of letters between the characters. Today, in the age of the telephone, the idea is unthinkable.

We now tend to write letters only when any other form of communication seems inappropriate; when we do not want an

immediate response; when an arrangement or contract is to be confirmed; or perhaps when we wish NOT to speak to the recipient!

As a result, writing has come to be seen as formal, or 'proper', requiring formal or 'proper' language that is somehow different from the language we use when speaking.

'Formal', though, does not mean 'impersonal'. We are responsible for every letter we sign: legally, and professionally. More than that, we all have individual styles which reflect our background and personality, and in professional letter-writing this personal element is increasingly important.

Why do letters fail?

We have all received letters which fail.

We have been addressed with the wrong name – or gender – or have been multiplied without our knowing it (*"Dear Sirs ..."*).

We have no idea what information the letter is attempting to convey, or, more importantly, what happens next. As the writer seems to have no idea who we are anyway, we hardly feel like finding out.

The letter is bedevilled with language which is old-fashioned, pompous, and reeking of officialdom. It is cramped on the page and poorly punctuated. As an ambassador for the writer and the organization whose letterhead sits proudly at the top of the page, it is clearly doing a poor job.

There are problems inherent in letters which we should recognize and allow for:

- We are not there to help the communication with our personality, with the tone of our voice or bodily gestures.
- There is a time problem. It takes time to write, and time to reply. We cannot get an immediate response; we cannot even be certain that the letter has arrived. And time is money.

Then there are *our* problems, as writers:

- We have not thought clearly about the message we want to send.
- We are not thinking of the reader, but of the material in the letter.
- We may not even be thinking of the contents of the letter, but only about which words will look impressive on the page.
- We are also thinking about the next letter, and the next, and all our other work, and the clock ...

The first set of problems, combined with the second, leads to:

- muddled thinking;
- a muddled structure (because our thinking is muddled);
- language that goes out of control because we are thinking as we write.

All of which wastes the reader's time, which is as valuable as ours, and destroys any hope of goodwill returning to us by the next post.

CHECKLIST: Why letters fail

WRITER	READER
■ Lack of purpose	■ Wrong address
■ Lack of confidence	■ Complicated words
■ No time	■ Impersonal
■ Problem of tone	■ Intimidating
■ Not knowing to whom to write	■ Poor layout
■ Poorly structured	■ No clear action
■ How to put thoughts into words?	■ Poor spelling
	■ Bad grammar
■ Cannot keep to the point	■ No heading
■ Sentences go out of control	■ Poor punctuation

Adopting a systematic approach

An effective business letter is precise, straightforward, relevant to the reader's needs, and action-centred. It shows respect for its reader and points the way ahead, saying clearly and unambiguously what happens next.

Writing effective letters is not some mysterious talent. It can be achieved by adopting a systematic approach, following a number of simple stages:

Preparation; Planning; Writing; Checking

This book is a guide through these stages. It takes you on a journey from an empty sheet of paper to a completed letter, signed, sealed and delivered.

Making letters work

CHECKLIST 1

- Letters express a relationship
- Formal but not impersonal

- *Why letters fail:*
  - lack of purpose
  - wrong reader
  - language problems
  - time problems

- *A systematic approach:*
  - preparation
  - planning
  - writing
  - checking

Preparation

Many writers describe the feeling of panic that hits them when confronting a blank sheet of paper. The reason for this disabling loss of confidence is really very simple: we have not prepared.

Even the simplest and briefest letter requires preparation. Longer, complicated or delicate letters will achieve their objective more effectively if time is spent preparing them before writing. Standard letters need to be prepared especially carefully if they are not to look impersonal.

To fail to prepare is to prepare to fail.

The basic questions

The best way to prepare is to ask a series of basic questions:

- Why?
- Who?
- When?
- Where?
- What?

In preparing to write, we are clarifying to ourselves the *purpose* of the letter and *to whom* it is being written. The time taken for the letter to arrive, and its destination – the *when* and *where* – are also of crucial importance.

Why?: the letter's purpose

Whether they are sent round the world or round the corner, letters should go on their way with a purpose. All too often they are sent on a wing and a prayer.

Try to establish the reason for writing the letter. Write it down as a simple verbal phrase:

- To get something done
- To confirm an agreement, appointment, contract
- To put a situation right: apologizing, repairing customer relations
- To persuade or sell: a product, service, or idea
- To give information: answering enquiries
- To get information
- To justify a course of action
- To explain a complex matter
- To report on progress
- To promote us and our organization

All these purposes are *actions*.

If your letter seems to have more than one purpose, pick the most important one, and stick to it. A letter which tries to do too much will fail to do anything.

Remember that all letters should act to promote us and our organization. Every letter we send is a free advertisement.

Expand your brief phrase into a *statement of purpose*, adding any detail specific to this letter. Write that statement on a piece of paper and keep it with you as you write the letter – it will help to concentrate your mind, especially if you get stuck!

- To urge a customer to settle an account
- To confirm a service contract for office cleaning
- To apologize for a missed delivery to a valued client
- To persuade a customer to investigate a new insurance policy
- To explain where to obtain a range of porcelain
- To recommend that new caterers are sought for the canteen
- To ask the Singapore office to send last year's figures
- To justify a disciplinary procedure
- To explain the workings of a new piece of equipment
- To report on progress in the departmental review

It is worth asking yourself, at this stage: "Why am I writing a *letter*?" A quick telephone call might clarify the matter immediately. On the other hand, the matter may be too serious to be dealt with by post – a meeting may be required.

Urgency may dictate the use of a fax. Although it is far faster than a letter, and may be laid out differently, a fax needs the same care and attention as any other document. The same applies to electronic mail. Do not be seduced by the technology into sloppiness which could cause problems later.

Who is the reader?

What we include in the letter – and leave out of it – will depend on our relationship with the reader.

Most importantly, are we writing to the *right* person? If we want something done, is the reader in a position to do it (or see it done)? The time taken to write and send the letter will be wasted if it is opened and read by the wrong person, particularly in a large organization. A quick telephone call to the department or switchboard could save much annoyance later.

Use the reader's *name* if at all possible. This can be difficult. We may be initiating a correspondence and have no contact name. We may be answering a letter signed with an initial and surname ("D. Smith"), or with an unfamiliar first name, neither of which tells us the writer's gender. Some writers give no indication of how they would prefer to be titled (Mrs? Miss? Ms?). The problem can be especially acute when dealing with large numbers of letters from the public, many of them handwritten.

We all know what it is like to receive a letter which names us wrongly, or makes assumptions about our gender or marital status. We should make every effort to address our reader by name, and get the reader's personal details right. In all these cases, a quick telephone call to the department or company switchboard could save much annoyance later.

Every reader has *needs* and *expectations*, which we should try to fulfil as best we can. Take care to omit information the reader does *not* want. Dissatisfied customers do not need lengthy explanations of the reasons for a breakdown in the computerized booking system: they want a prompt refund.

We may, of course, not be able to satisfy our reader. They may want what they cannot have (a model that is no longer available; a job) or they may need what they do not want (a new set of regulations; a gentle reminder). In either case, if we are at least aware of potential difficulties, we will be able to employ diplomacy or tact as appropriate.

Behind every writer and reader is a mass of *attitudes*. Does the situation have a 'history'? Can we glean anything about our reader from past letters, or from our colleagues? Do we represent an organization or profession with a particular public image or reputation? How could we turn any of our reader's attitudes to our advantage?

Consider, too, the reader's *level of knowledge*: of us, of our organization, and of the complexity of the situation. We may be writing to a colleague we have known for years, or to a member of the public we will never meet. If in doubt, explain more rather than less, and pitch your expression a little 'low'. Nobody will be insulted by clear explanations and straightforward language.

Remember to mark all *confidential* mail clearly and consider whether a letter is adequately secure as a means of communicating any delicate information.

Will our letter have more than one reader? *Mailshots* and *standard letters* should be drafted carefully. Research is particularly important in this area. It may be necessary to break the readership into groups with different letters for each.

CHECKLIST: The reader

- The right person?
- Authority? The decision-maker? The action-taker?
- How well known to me: Colleague? Opposite number? Supplier/contractor? Customer?
- Name: job title?

■ Wants/needs? What do they NOT want/need?
■ What do they know about us, the organization, the situation?
■ What is their attitude?
■ What is their level of understanding?
■ Confidentiality?
■ More than one reader? – mailshots; standard letters

Who? Me?

Am I the right person to be writing this letter?

Perhaps it is my job to liaise between my organization and the public. It may be my responsibility to find the information I am looking for, or to see that a contract is satisfactorily completed. I may be the expert.

Letters are unfortunately sometimes delegated to writers who have neither the authority nor the information to write them. We *must* know enough to be able to draft the letter correctly, and should have the authority to carry out any action indicated in the letter, especially when giving a warning or threatening legal action.

Remember that the person signing the letter is legally responsible for its contents, even when signing 'pp', or on behalf of a colleague, *unless* the signature is accompanied by the disclaimer: "Dictated by ... and signed in their absence".

CHECKLIST: The writer

■ The right person?
■ Our authority?
■ Our credibility?
■ Our level of knowledge?
■ Our access to information?
■ Can we take responsibility for the letter?

When?

Letters take time to arrive. Even faxes have been known to sit in the post room for several hours.

We cannot be certain exactly when our letter will reach its reader. It must be given time to be delivered, and the reader time to reply – especially if deadlines for action are involved. Do not give the reader the excuse that the letter didn't arrive in time.

On the other hand, the letter must clearly be up-to-date: there is no point in sending it so early that crucial information must be left out, or so late that we are overtaken by events.

It may be worth calling the reader by telephone to signal that an important letter is on the way. Faxes should certainly be confirmed by phone, to speed retrieval.

Give yourself time to write, and time to check, the letter. Try to manage your time so that you write when your mind is fresh. You will probably clear your correspondence more quickly and efficiently if you deal with it all first thing in the morning.

Be aware of all the methods of despatch available to you. The extra cost of a courier may be beneficial if it gives you a little longer to draft an urgent letter – though it may be difficult to convince the accounts department of this!

CHECKLIST: When?

- Deliver in good time
- Give reader time to reply
- Allow for weekends and holidays
- Anticipate deadlines
- Up-to-date information

- Confirm important letter or fax by phone
- Give yourself time to write – and check
- Time management: write when fresh
- Method of despatch: time benefit?

Where?

All our hard work will be in vain if the letter misses its destination.

If we know the reader's name, we should also know their *exact address*. Make sure that it is up-to-date: people are promoted and replaced. They move between departments or retire. Organizations sometimes spread over various sites; companies relocate, expand or 'rationalize'.

Letters going abroad may need to be translated, and will need to be addressed appropriately.

Give thought to where you will be writing. Is it somewhere convenient, quiet, conducive to thought and free from interruptions?

If not, is there anything you can do to improve matters?

Do not feel bound to your desk. Some letters are written in the canteen, some in the staff lavatory! Ten minutes' quiet thinking somewhere else can be ten minutes well spent, especially if you are stuck.

CHECKLIST: Where?

- Exact address: including department, room number, site?
- Full address: including postcode?
- Is the reader there?
- Abroad? Translation? Style of address? Method of despatch?

- Where to write:
  - close to information
  - quiet
  - free from interruptions
- If in difficulty, think away from the desk

Only when these four basic questions are answered – *Why? Who? When? Where?* – will you be ready to begin drafting your letter. The *What?* and the *How?* – what to put in it, and how to express it – will follow.

If you are unsure about something, ask. A mistake or an omission at this stage is easily corrected; once sent, a letter is irretrievable.

Time spent on preparation is time saved later in writing the letter – and in reading it at the other end. Getting our message clear in the reader's mind depends on getting it clear in ours first.

Preparation

CHECKLIST 2

The basic questions:

- Why?
  - purpose of letter: statement of purpose: action
  - why a letter?
- Who is the reader?
  - the right person?
  - name?
  - needs and expectations?
  - confidentiality?

- ■ Who is the writer?
  - – function?
  - – knowledge and authority?
- ■ When?
  - – deadlines?
  - – when to write?
- ■ Where?
  - – letter's destination?
  - – where to write?

Planning

The action point

What will happen as a result of our letter?

Our statement of purpose centres on a specific *action* which will be carried out either by us, or by our reader. Put another way, the *action point* of the letter is whatever needs to be done in order to fulfil the letter's purpose.

Possible action points for the *writer* might include:

- visiting a client;
- making a refund;
- getting a job interview;
- supplying vital information in order to complete a project.

Possible action points for the *reader* might include:

- completion of work by a contractor to agreed specifications, by an agreed date;

- a meeting: at an agreed venue, date and time;
- Buying one of our products;
- Supplying figures in order to complete the yearly report.

The action point is the most important part of the letter. Everything else in the letter should contribute to it, and be planned around it.

We must now ask a number of *What?* questions:

- What ACTION is required? By whom? When?
- What information is RELEVANT to the action point?
- What knowledge does the reader already have?
- What do I already know?
- What else do I need?
- Where do I go to get it?

We may attempt to answer these questions by making a list of points. However, there is an easier, quicker and more efficient method of gathering and ordering the material we will require in order to write the letter.

Pattern planning: an example

Imagine we are writing to a theatre to book tickets. Telephone bookings are not accepted.

Instead of listing all the information we require, we might pattern plan it. We draw a circle in the centre of a piece of paper, and write the action point in it: "Book theatre seats."

We then write down all the information we need in order to make the booking: in any order, as it comes to us, all over the page. We might draw pictures or symbols to act as memory joggers. It is crucial to include everything that comes to mind, even if it may not seem relevant.

The items of information are then grouped together, and anything not strictly necessary to the letter can be deleted. Actually it will probably have sorted itself into groups to some extent, and only a little deleting and moving of items will be necessary.

Finally, we list the groups in a logical sequence, assigning a number to each.

We have produced a simple pattern plan: an increasingly popular method of organizing information.

Our culture encourages us to think in lists: hierarchies of information, categories, logical sequences, cause and effect. Society could not function without such thinking. But lists are limiting: like tramlines, they force us to think only of a few things at a time, and order material in ways which may not be appropriate.

Pattern plans allow us to access information in our minds far more quickly and completely than lists. They have a number of clear advantages as thinking tools:

- rapidity: we are allowed to think freely, getting ideas onto the page more quickly;
- completeness: we can see the whole at a glance, and are less likely to leave something out by mistake;
- efficiency: they gather the material and order it *at the same time.*

Perhaps most importantly, pattern plans are *individual.* We all think differently, making connections between ideas according to our needs, taste and experience. Material organized in a pattern plan will make sense to us, and so have a far better chance of making sense to our reader.

Any letter can be planned in this way. The simpler the letter, the quicker the planning process will be. A longer, more complex letter will benefit immensely from a pattern plan:

- the material will be ordered far more quickly into sections;
- each section can be given a heading;
- the items in each section can be arranged logically;
- material can be edited for relevance;
- omissions will be obvious at an early stage.

At the end of this process, our material, complete, edited for relevance to the action point, and in order, is ready to be structured as a letter.

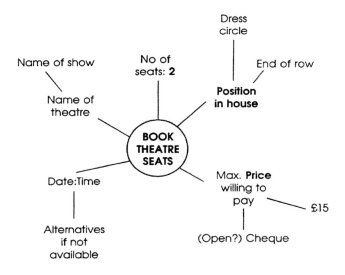

Planning

CHECKLIST 3

- Establish the action point of the letter
- What information is relevant to the action point?
- What do I know? What do I need to know?
- Pattern plan the material: put in order

Structure

Every letter needs a structure: it saves time and confusion.

The material in almost all business letters follows this basic format:

- Salutation
- Introduction
- Body
- Action point
- Concluding remarks
- Complimentary close (or subscription)

Salutation

Countless books have been written on the subject of etiquette in letter writing. Usage has become more relaxed of recent years, and a few basic rules will suffice for most business situations.

If you know the reader's name, use it. We are writing to an individual, not to an organization.

The form of the name you choose depends on how the reader has signed any letters to you, on how well you know each other, and on your own taste. Business contacts, even if they have never previously corresponded or met, increasingly salute each other by first name:

Dear Michael ...
Dear Sonia ...

The more formal style of salutation is normally reserved for members of the public and customers of various kinds:

Dear Mr Brown ...
Dear Mrs Wilson ...
Dear Miss Farthingale ...
Dear Ms Wright ...

If the marital status of a female reader is unclear, and you cannot use her first name, we recommend the use of *Ms*. Note, however, that it is not yet universally acceptable in business – or anywhere else!

A correspondent signing a letter with an initial and last name (*D Smith*) should, say some authorities, be styled as such at the beginning of the letter. This seems unnecessarily impersonal and old-fashioned. Unless research can clarify the matter, you may have to resort to one of:

Dear Sir ...
Dear Madam ...
Dear Sir or Madam ...

But avoid these if at all possible. The following should be avoided at all costs:

Sir ...
Madam ...
My Dear Sir ...
Dear Sirs ...
Dear Mesdames ...
Gentlemen ...
My Dear Mr Ferguson ...
Dear Ferguson ...
My Dear Ferguson ...

If in doubt phone to check the reader's preferred style of address.

Heading

Any business letter benefits from a heading. It acts as a signpost, focusing the reader's attention immediately on the letter's subject.

As the letter deals with one subject, it should be possible to sum it up in a single, brief phrase. Ensure that the heading is as meaningful to the reader as it is to us. *'Invoice No. 431298'* may mean very little; *'Installation of new kitchen units'* is more helpful.

Re: siting of street lamps in Wentworth Street is a more formal style of heading and may be preferred by some organizations.

The heading is placed between the salutation and the introduction. A heading makes it much easier to start the letter with a short first sentence:

INVOICE No. 431298: Installation of new kitchen units
Thank you for your enquiry.
Re: Siting of street lamps in Wentworth Street
Many thanks for your letter.

Introduction

The first paragraph of the letter should clearly identify:

- an acknowledgement of any previous communication (with date);
- who the writer is;
- why you are writing.

The reader should know as soon as possible why the letter has been written and what it is about.

Take care to avoid opening letters in ways that are verbose, old-fashioned or grammatically incorrect:

With reference to your enquiry of 17th July.
Further to our telephone conversation of 23rd December.
Following numerous telephone calls to your site management, and the lack of response to our requests for urgent updates in

connection with our contract with you to build a warehouse at our Uxbridge site, for completion on the 1 July 1992.

All three of these openings – from real letters – are grammatically wrong. They are not sentences.

Begin simply:

Thank you for your letter of 30 January.
I refer to your letter of 30th January.

These are both acceptable openings: simple, straightforward, polite. The first is preferable; the second is rather formal.

Letters initiating contact, and beginning *I am writing ...* – which is stating the obvious – might more effectively open by referring to what the writer wants, or is about to do:

I am concerned ...
I am interested in ...
I saw your advertisement ...
I understand that you are interested in ...
I have recently taken up the post of ... and have pleasure in ...

If you are using *We* instead of *I*, be clear who exactly you mean: the team, the department, the company, the trade union membership, the profession. On the whole, any letter should speak for the writer alone.

Body

This is the meat of the letter. Ensure that all the material is relevant to the action point and logically ordered. Give paragraphs sub-headings if it will help the reader understand complex material.

The body of the letter is made up of facts, explanations and possibly opinions. The language, structure and tone used to present them are discussed in Chapter 6.

Action point

This is the most important part of the letter. If the reader misses this, the letter will have failed.

Isolate the action point by placing it in a paragraph on its own. If appropriate, print it in **bold type** or *italics*.

Any action point should indicate:

- what action needs to be taken;
- when it is to be taken;
- who is responsible for taking it.

Be careful not to be too abrupt in your demands, or too effusive in your promises. Actions should be specific and realistic.

Concluding remarks

The last sentence of the letter is as important as the first. We are setting the seal on the relationship – it is essential to leave our reader with the correct impression.

Avoid the stale and standard remark:

Thanking you in anticipation ...
I look forward to hearing from you at your earliest convenience.
Assuring you of our best attention at all times ...
I have the honour to be, with great truth and respect, Sir, your obedient servant ...
I avail myself of this opportunity to renew to Your Excellency the assurance of my highest consideration ...

In the meantime, if you have any queries, please do not hesitate to contact me.

The last example has become such a cliché that the reader will not know whether it is a genuine invitation or not. Of course we must be polite, but such phrases indicate a lack of care rather than an individual response.

We can be polite and genuine:

I can be contacted on the above number if you have any queries.
I look forward to hearing from you.
Please call me on ... if you need help.
I hope this information is helpful.

Think about what you would say face to face, and put it into a form acceptable at the end of a letter.

The complimentary close and signature

The rule is very simple.

All business letters should end in one of two ways:

Dear Sir
Dear Madam   *Yours faithfully*
Dear Sir or Madam

Dear Derek
Dear Joanna
Dear Mr Brown   *Yours sincerely*
Dear Ms Wellington
Dear Mrs Whitbread

Use *Yours faithfully* when you do not salute the reader by name. Otherwise use *Yours sincerely*.

Note the use of capital letters: for *Yours* only.

Other complimentary closes will suggest other types of relationships, none of them entirely or solely professional:

Yours
Yours ever
Yours very sincerely
Sincerely
Kind regards
As ever
Yours affectionately

... and so on. Use them at your own risk!

Sign with your first name if you have saluted the reader by first name, otherwise with your first and last names (*not* an initial and last name). Never include your title (*Mr/Mrs/Miss/Ms*) in the signature itself.

It is standard practice in business to type or print the writer's name and job title below the signature. The signature and printed name must correspond exactly, with the proviso that the printed name can include a personal title. The job title is printed under the printed name. Either name or job title – but not both – can be printed in upper case.

Yours sincerely

Bridget O'Hare (Mrs)
PERSONNEL DIRECTOR

Remember the old rule: do as you would be done by. If we fail to sign ourselves as we would wish to be addressed, we have only ourselves to blame if we take offence at a letter which addresses us incorrectly.

Structure

CHECKLIST 4

- Salutation: by name if possible
- First name for many business contacts: surname for public and new customers
- Give the letter a heading
- Short, personal introduction
- Body of the letter well paragraphed and laid out
- Action point: isolate in its own paragraph; highlighted
- Concluding remarks: polite but genuine
- Yours faithfully/sincerely
- Print full name and job title under the signature

Layout

A letter begins its work as ambassador the moment it arrives.

The look of the envelope is the very first impression the reader has of the writer. The layout of the letter itself immediately indicates the attitude of the writer to the task of communicating, and to the reader.

However well-written, a letter which is poorly presented will fail at the first hurdle.

Styles of layout

Most business letters come in one of four layouts:

■ *Indented*
  – Addresses and close/signature progressively indented;
  – heading, writer's name and job title centred;
  – closed punctuation (commas and stops in names and addresses, dates, complimentary close).

Now regarded as old-fashioned, largely because of the complexity of typing. Not recommended.

■ *Blocked*
  – everything starting at the left margin;
  – open punctuation (all punctuation omitted outside the main body of the letter).

Far easier and quicker to produce; very common.

■ *Semi-blocked*
  – everything starts at the left margin except:
  date and complimentary close on the right;
  – heading centred.

Has the advantage of balancing the page somewhat. The date on the right assists retrieval from files.

■ *Semi-indented*
  – like semi-blocked except:
  paragraphs indented.

Only marginally preferable to fully indented.

It must be said that there is no absolute agreement about any of the details in these layouts.

FLUSTER, BLUSTER, CRUSTER & QUALM
Chartered Charterers of Repute
Lincolns Inn, LONDON WC1

Our ref.:   6th. July, 19..
Your ref.:

The Information Officer,
  Messrs. Reader and Reader,
    Derrydown Road,
      ANYTOWN,
        Greenshire,
          AY99 3FR.

Dear Sir or Madam,

The Indented Letter

With reference to your esteemed enquiry of the 1st. inst., we beg to present an example of the traditional, fully indented layout of business communication.

We would draw to your attention the following features of this letter:

1. As you will see, your address, the complimentary close and the signature have all been progressively indented.
2. Each paragraph is indented.
3. The heading of the letter, together with the writer's name and job title, are centred;
4. The date of the letter is placed on the right-hand side.
5. Closed punctuation is used in the address, the salutation, and the complimentary close.

These features, together with our somewhat antiquated mode of expression, contribute to an overall effect of fustiness.

I have the honour to be your most humble servant,

Ethelred Cobweb
Assistant Senior Secretary

INTERNATIONAL COMMUNICATIONS plc
Quotient House, Broadway, GILLINGHAM GA77 3FF

Our ref:
Your ref:

6 July 19..

Bena Patel
Reader and Reader
Derrydown Road
ANYTOWN
Greenshire
AY99 3FR

Dear Bena

The Fully blocked Letter

Thank you for your letter of 1 July. This is an example of the blocked style of letter which you asked about.

As you can see, everything in this letter starts at the left margin.

Punctuation is open: only essential dots and commas are

included. All this makes the letter much easier (and quicker!) to type. Most business letters are now laid out in this style. It is efficient and modern.

My own feeling, however, is that fully blocked letters can sometimes look rather lopsided. This impression would be reinforced if I had had to type my own name and address above yours at the head of the letter.

Some writers prefer to right justify, that is, to make a straight margin at the right-hand side. I feel that a 'ragged' edge on the right makes the letter look more personal.

I hope that this answers your questions, and that my tone strikes you as friendly. If you would like to discuss this matter further, please contact me on the above number.

Yours sincerely

John Hopkins
Communications Administrator

INFORMATION FOR BUSINESS
The Arden Centre, Fourways, Edgbaston, BIRMINGHAM B98 6CX

Our ref:
Your ref:

6 July 19..

Roger Williams
Reader and Reader
Derrydown Road
ANYTOWN
Greenshire
AY99 3FR

Dear Roger

<u>The Semi-blocked Letter</u>

You asked me to clarify the matter of semi-blocked layout.

Quite a few organizations are adapting this layout to create letters combining the modern 'look' with a few extra useful features.

There are two points to notice in this letter:

1. The date, references, close, writer's name and job title are all on the right. This makes for ease of retrieval from files.
2. The heading of the letter is centred, for greater emphasis.

Everything else starts at the left margin. All paragraphs are blocked.

These features give a more balanced look on the page. The letter can be typed fairly efficiently, but the effect is not so fussy as a letter fully indented.

I hope this is of some help.

Yours sincerely

Allan Order
Data Manager

INFORMATION FOR BUSINESS
The Arden Centre, Fourways, Edgbaston, BIRMINGHAM B98 6CX

Our ref:
Your ref:

6 July 19..

Roger Williams
Reader and Reader
Derrydown Road
ANYTOWN
Greenshire
AY99 3FR

Dear Roger

The Semi-indented Letter

Thank you for your call. I appreciate that I failed to mention the semi-indented style of letter, so here is an example.

This letter is essentially exactly the same as a semi-blocked letter. The only difference is that the paragraphs are indented.

Personally I can't see the point of it. Some people may prefer the slightly more 'formal' impression of this letter, but as far as I can see it just makes for a few more seconds' typing which could be spent doing something more useful.

There really are no more styles of letter writing that I know of, so I would welcome your not asking me any more questions about them. Your own company should have guidelines to help you draft your letters, and beyond that it really is a matter of personal taste.

Yours sincerely

Allan Order
Data Manager

Once you have chosen a style of layout, or adopted the company's style, use it consistently throughout each letter.

The letterhead

It is very rare that an organization will not use a printed letterhead. It should include:

- the organization's name or company trading name;
- address, including postcode;
- telephone, telex and fax numbers;
- status as a limited company if appropriate.

It will probably also include a logo.

In order to complement a blocked or semi-blocked layout, the letterhead should be either centred or weighted to the right; the printed 'home' name and address then balances the recipient's name and address on the left.

If our own name and address are to be typed onto an unheaded page of blocked or semi-blocked layout, they must go at the top right.

References

References allow for easy filing and tracing of letters. They are normally composed of:

- initials of writer (capitals);
- initials of typist (sometimes in lower case);
- reference to a particular file, account, invoice, etc. (if relevant)

When replying to a referenced letter, quote both references, in the following order:

Our ref: AB/PR/CF4
Your ref: FG/kj

References are placed above the date in all layouts except the fully indented.

The date

Every letter should be dated, including standard or circular letters.

Use a clean, uncluttered form: *st, th, rd* are increasingly omitted, and commas and stops should not be used with open punctuation and blocked layout.

Abbreviations (*Jan, '92*) are unsuitable for letters, as are numerical forms of the date (*23/5/92*).

The recommended date form is:

1 April 1992

Reader's name and address

Blocked or indented, with open or closed punctuation, as appropriate:

Mr G D Smith   *Ms. S. Ritter,*
Technical Director   *Personnel Manager,*
Boltaway Mouldings plc   *W. D. Crank & Sons, Ltd.,*
34 Field Road   *465 Bleek Avenue,*
HALLINGFORD   *JESSLEY*
Lincolnshire   *Lancashire*
LN67 8RF   *BL96 3VB*

If using a 'window' envelope, you may need to restrict the name and address to four or five lines. The postcode can be placed on the same line as the county, with a suitable gap; county names are sometimes unnecessary for big towns or cities (but check which ones) and the job title can be omitted if absolutely necessary.

After the close

There are a few elements which sometimes follow the signature and typed name and job title.

- *PS*, or *P.S.*, is by no means unacceptable in a business letter. It does not necessarily suggest laziness or sloppy thinking; indeed, it can be a useful way of highlighting a particular bit of information, or reminding the reader of a small point. If genuine, it adds a friendly tone to the letter. Some circulars use the device to fabricate friendliness, adding exclamation marks, *PPS* and so on. Be aware of the effect *PS* will have and use it appropriately.
- *Enc.*, or *Encs 3*, indicate papers enclosed with the letter. Sometimes a slash (/) is placed in the margin beside the reference to the enclosure in the text. A description of the enclosures is helpful for both typist and reader:

  Encs: 1993 brochure
  Company sales figures 1990–1
  Invoice No 098765

- Copies of the letter to third parties are indicated by *Copy to*, *Copies to*, or *cc*, with relevant names added.

The envelope

Every day the Post Office handles some five million letters which are wrongly addressed.

The Post Office makes the following recommendations about addressing envelopes:

- Leave at least 4 cm at the top of the envelope for the postmark and stamps;
- Reader's full address, including post town, county name and postcode, except for cities and large towns;
- Post town to be written in BLOCK CAPITALS;
- Postcode in block capitals, no punctuation, on a separate line if possible;
- Nothing to be typed under the postcode.

A few further tips:

- Type the envelope as you type the letter. If the letter cannot be signed and sealed immediately, enclose or attach it to the envelope, to avoid confusion.
- Lay out the envelope consistently with the letter: indented (double spaced) or blocked (single spaced).
- Name your readers *exactly* as they have signed themselves. Be sure to spell the name correctly.
- *Street; Avenue; Road* to be typed in full.
- Mark the envelope *Confidential* or *Personal* in the top left-hand corner, 4 cm from the top edge.
- When using a 'window' envelope, make sure that the full name and address, including the postcode, are visible.
- Check the name and address against the name and address on the letter, and against any correspondence from the reader.

■ The sender's corporate name and address should be printed on every envelope sent out. It will ensure that you keep in contact with any letters that fail to get through – and is free publicity.

Your organization may publish guidelines on the house style of written documents, including the layout of letters. Agreed standards of practice may be handed down within a department in an informal manner.

Do not ignore house-style. You may one day be called upon to revise it. It is worthwhile, too, comparing your organization's style with that of others whose letters you see – at work or at home.

Once you start looking, you will notice that letters vary remarkably in their visual impact. Take note of good ideas, and put them into practice in your own letters.

Layout

CHECKLIST 5

■ Styles: indented, blocked, semi-indented, semi-blocked
■ Be consistent
■ Clean, uncluttered date form
■ References
■ Addressee's name and address
■ Lay out the envelope correctly

Writing

Letter writing is 'a piece of conversation by post'. Yet many people still put words and phrases into letters that they would never dream of saying to someone.

The formality of the letter lies in its structure and in a few basic conventions of politeness. In every other respect, the language we use should be as close to the spoken word as possible.

There is no such thing as 'business English': there is only good English. Beware of writing in a certain way because it seems more 'businesslike' or 'correct'. Be guided by the preparatory questions you asked yourself:

■ the letter's purpose;
■ your relationship with the reader.

Review the material you have gathered to put in the letter, and the *action* that will follow. The task now is to put that material down on paper in language that is *accurate, brief* and *clear.*

Words and phrases

Accuracy means using the right word for the right job.

Language changes over time. Words appropriate in a letter thirty years ago may now be old-fashioned. Avoid words such as:

Herewith
Aforesaid
Furthermore
Whereas
Undermentioned
Inasmuch

Replace phrases such as:

We beg to acknowledge receipt of ...
Your letter of the 3rd inst. is to hand ...
I am writing in furtherance of our recent communication ...

– with simpler, more straightforward ones:

Thank you for ...
Your letter of 3 August has been passed to me ...
I am happy to confirm the arrangement made by telephone ...

Words lose meanings and acquire new ones. Changes in technology or working practices can create new vocabularies. A *disc* in the 1960s was something very different from a *disk* in the 1990s.

All professions or business communities use *jargon*: words which have a specific and limited meaning within that community, but which, to an outsider, are meaningless.

Jargon has its place. A letter to a fellow expert can usefully employ specialized terminology to provide clearer and quicker communication. For non-specialists, however, jargon should be kept to a minimum.

There are other kinds of private languages in business: *'buzz words'* used between colleagues (and competitors!) to suggest status, trendiness, membership of the clique. In letters they can create confusion, annoyance, and antagonism. Say what you mean: not what you think will look good.

Brevity means using the short word rather than the long one. Do not 'endeavour to ascertain' – try to find out. Why 'utilise' when you can use, or 'facilitate' when you can make easier?

If a word says what you want to say, accurately and briefly, use it. If it adds nothing to the meaning, cut it out.

Sometimes whole phrases can be dispensed with. The word *cliché* derives from printing – originally it was the metal stereotype from which an engraving was printed. Now it refers to stereotyped phrases, words which go about glued together in blocks, clogging the language.

Clichés are a form of automatic writing – they betray a lack of thinking. They often appear in letters because the task of writing them is often necessarily repetitive.

Some clichés can be replaced with simpler words and phrases:

We will explore every avenue	:	*We will try*
in this day and age	:	*now*
in view of the fact that	:	*because*
plus the fact that	:	*and*
in the first place	:	*first*

Others mean nothing at all. Hunt down and exterminate phrases such as:

as a matter of fact	*fact of the matter*
as a rule	*for the time being*
as such	*for your information*
at all events	*in any shape or form*
axe to grind	*better half*
be that as it may	*bear in mind*
bound to admit	*last but not least*
by and large	*needless to say*
by the way	*on the contrary*
conspicuous by its absence	*plus the fact that*
each and every one of us	*in terms of*
to all intents and purposes	*unparalleled success*

Tautology means repetition, and is another enemy to brevity. Why say the same thing twice?

He declined to <u>accept</u> our offer.
Enclosed <u>herewith</u> …
The <u>true</u> facts are …
In <u>close</u> proximity …
A <u>joint</u> collaboration …

I <u>myself</u> ...
Often <u>in the habit of</u> ...
The reason is <u>because</u> ...
Giving <u>mutual</u> help ...

All the words underlined above are tautologous, and should be cut out. Tautologies can be difficult to spot, and often arise through a concern for formality.

Clarity is a matter of leaving no room for ambiguity or wrong assumptions. You must know the facts, and state them precisely.

Vague phrases arouse the reader's suspicion:

in the region of
in the area of
around about
a certain amount of

Is the writer covering up something unpleasant, or simply masking ignorance?

Beware, too, of **redundant words**:

<u>most</u> *perfect*
<u>quite</u> *unique*
<u>very</u> *excellent*

Perfect, unique and **excellent** express the highest degree of a quality: **most, quite, very,** have no meaning attached to them.

Loaded words convey value judgements which may not be intended. During a staff survey, a person may have been *approached, asked a question, questioned, interviewed,* or even *interrogated*: the implications of the manner in which they have been treated will differ in each case.

The greatest threat to clarity in letters comes from *abstract words*. Concepts are far less easy to grasp than concrete, descriptive words, which the reader can visualize.

There are regulations for the <u>avoidance</u> of accidents.
Your <u>entitlement</u> to a refund is not affected by this clause.
We have <u>pleasure in announcing</u> the appointment of a new Chairman.

The sentences above will be clearer and more straightforward if the underlined abstract words are replaced with concrete ones:

We have rules which help us avoid accidents.
You are still entitled to a refund.
We are pleased to announce that Mr X is our new Chairman.

Concrete words name things (and people) clearly, simplify the use of language, and will probably mean the same to the reader as to the writer. They also help to make sentences shorter.

CHECKLIST: Words

■ Accurate:	Old-fashioned language
	Old/new meanings
	Jargon in its proper place
	Buzz words: in-house or professional terminology
■ Brief:	Short words instead of long ones
	Clichés
	Tautology (the reason is because)
■ Clear:	Vague words (in the region of)
	Redundant words (most perfect)
	Loaded words
	Abstract words

Sentences

Short sentences are easier to read than long ones.

We are trained, when reading, to stop and absorb information fully only when we come to a full stop. If we cannot stop and absorb, we must go on, 'mopping up' whatever we can, until finally we are forced to give up and take another run at the sentence.

Use your shortest sentences in prominent positions: at the beginning of the letter, and at the end. Paragraphs should begin with short sentences, and benefit from ending with them.

The most important words in the sentence are best placed at the beginning and the end, where they will be registered most strongly.

Ideas can often find themselves isolated within sentences. The connections between them – association, logical progression, or contrast – should be expressed by link words or phrases, and by punctuation.

Link words and phrases include:

- In addition
- In contrast to
- On the other hand
- At the same time
- Bearing in mind
- Nevertheless
- As a result
- However

But, and, therefore and *also* are powerful linking words, but should not, as a rule, begin a sentence.

Tautology can afflict sentences as well as words. Writers sometimes feel that an important idea must be stated twice if it is to make its effect. Not so. The bigger the idea, the more simply it must be expressed.

Sentences grow out of control when we try to cram too many ideas into them. We are thinking and writing at the same time. The only answer is to separate thought from writing.

Sentence analysis: an example

Any sentence of 25 words or more should be analysed and reconstructed. This can be done simply by cutting out clichés, tautologies, vague or redundant words, and so on. With monster sentences, a better method is to employ a four-point plan:

1. List the ideas in the sentence, reordering if necessary to make logical sense.
2. Rewrite each idea as a separate sentence.
3. Connect into prose, using link words or phrases or punctuation if necessary.
4. Check language for accuracy, brevity and clarity.

This is a sentence (from a real letter) which urgently needs to be rewritten!

I formally now inform you that we are taking delivery of a large consignment of materials from Germany in the second week of July to the value of £500,000 and should there not be any warehouse facilities available for the protection of these materials we will hold you and your company responsible for all damages occurred to these, and the subsequent claims from our customers for failure to supply, on top of the damages for non-completion of contract between us. [80 words]

There is no one way to do this! A possible solution might be as follows:

1. Ideas in the sentence:
a. Formal warning.
b. Delivery from Germany: second week of July: large consignment: value £500,000.
c. If the warehouse is not available to store this consignment, your company will be liable for:
 – damages to goods;
 – claims from our customers;
 – damages for non-completion of contract.
2. Rewrite each idea as a separate sentence:
a. This letter is a formal warning.
b. We are expecting a delivery of goods from Germany in the second week of July, to the value of £500,000.
c. If the warehouse is not available for use by then, we will hold your company liable for:
a) any damage caused to the goods;
b) any claims made against us by our customers;
c) damages for non-completion of contract.
3. Connect into prose, using links as necessary:
We are now regretfully obliged to issue you with a formal warning. We are expecting a delivery of goods from Germany in the second week of July, to the value of £500,000. If the warehouse is not available for use by then, we will hold your company liable for any damage caused to the goods, any claims made against us by our customers, and damages for non-completion of contract.
4. Check language for accuracy, brevity, clarity:
■ Are all the delivery details relevant?
■ *Regretfully obliged, issue you with* are clichés.
■ *Damage* repeated with two senses: causes confusion.

■ The liability more effective if tabulated.

The final version reads:

We must now give you a formal warning. We expect a delivery of goods in the second week of July, to the value of £500,000. If the warehouse is not available for use by then, your company will be liable for:

a) any damage caused to the goods;
b) any claims made against us by our customers;
c) agreed compensation for non-completion of contract.

Such sentence analysis may seem time-consuming at first, but it must be done. With practice it will become second nature and if it saves the annoyance of explanatory telephone calls later, it is worth the trouble.

CHECKLIST: Sentences

■ Short easier to read than long
■ Should vary in length
■ None longer than 25 words
■ Big idea: short sentence
■ Introduction of idea or section: short sentence
■ Summary of idea or section: short sentence
■ Strong places in sentence: beginning and end
■ Connect sentences with link words and punctuation

■ Long sentence (over 25 words)?
  – list ideas, reordering for sense
  – rewrite each idea as a separate sentence
  – connect into prose, using link words or phrases or punctuation
  – check language for accuracy, brevity and clarity

Paragraphs

Paragraphs present information on *one* aspect of a subject. They may have more than one sentence; they will only ever have one theme.

Like the heading of the letter, paragraphs are signposts, guiding the reader's eye down the page. The introduction of the letter should be contained in a short paragraph, and the action point isolated in its own paragraph.

The first, short sentence of each paragraph should summarize the whole paragraph: by skimming down the page, the reader can then pick up from these *topic sentences* the gist of the whole letter.

Use link words at the beginning of each paragraph to guide the reader from one idea to the next.

CHECKLIST: Paragraphs

- Usually more than one sentence: only one theme
- Short paragraph for introduction
- Highlight action point by isolating it in a paragraph
- Sub-headings and/or numbers for paragraphs in complex letters
- Short summary sentence at beginning of each paragraph
- Connect paragraphs with link words and phrases

Tone

Tone is difficult to define. We may have ordered our material logically, structured the letter properly, and written in language that is splendidly accurate, brief and clear, but the wrong tone will produce an effect very different from what we intend.

There are three elements which contribute crucially to good tone. We must:

BE POSITIVE: BE DEFINITE: BE SINCERE

- *Be definite:* do not promise what you cannot deliver.

We are unable to provide the goods before 15 September.
We will be able to supply these goods on 15th September.

The second sentence is guaranteed to produce a better response than the first.

- *Be definite:* do not promise what you cannot deliver.

I will try to ensure that the tickets are held for you.
I will hold the tickets for three days.

- *Be sincere:* generate in your reader the feeling appropriate to the purpose of the letter, and do not cloud your message with emotive language which the reader might interpret as a personal attack.

Your failure to reply ...
Your refusal to co-operate ...
It surprises me that someone of your intelligence should have misunderstood the terms of the policy so completely.

All these examples should be replaced with language which is sincere but also positive and definite – in a word, *professional.*

I have not yet received a reply ...
As you feel that we should not continue to work together ...
I would be delighted to talk to you again to clarify any matters in the policy which may be unclear.

Slang and colloquialisms in letters are to be avoided, as are jokes (although humour can enliven an ordinary letter), and foreign words used for effect. Abbreviations should be employed sparingly: for *e.g.* or *i.e.,* the words in full are neater.

Beware of writing impersonally.
Arrangements <u>have been made</u> to replace these goods.
Measurements <u>were taken</u> at various stages ...
Supplies <u>are expected</u> ...
Although small remittances <u>have been forwarded to us</u> ...
All letters <u>should be addressed</u> to me personally ...

This use of the impersonal, *passive voice* lacks the warm, friendly tone that is the mark of good business relations. It also complicates the letter's language. Most importantly, it fails to allocate responsibility for actions taken or to be taken.

Impersonal statements can create meanings you do not intend. *I do not believe* is substantially different from *It is not to be believed.*

Change passive verbs into *active verbs*, which tell the reader who is doing what:

I have replaced these goods and sent them to you.
The team measured the gas flow several times ...
We expect supplies of these goods ...
You have certainly sent us some sums in part-payment ...
Please address all letters to me at the above address.

CHECKLIST: Tone

- POSITIVE: DEFINITE: SINCERE
- Objective of letter?
- Relationship to reader?
- Avoid slang, colloquialisms

- No jokes (but consider humour)
- No foreign words for effect
- Take care with abbreviations
- Active voice, not passive

Beware of blind imitation in your letters. Find the mode of expression which is appropriate to you. Welcome help, but resist imposed alterations. Nobody is more useful than a trusted colleague who can give unbiased suggestions and practical examples; the manager who wields a red pen without explanation should be challenged.

Every letter's tone will differ according to the situation and the writer. You will not develop your own style overnight. Tackle a small part of every letter you write. Practise the skills of choosing words, constructing sentences and building paragraphs. They will become habitual.

A good writer feeds on other writing – stealing ideas from colleagues, studying the literature produced by the organization and devouring print at every opportunity. Everything is grist to the writer's mill: magazines, books, letters in the local newspaper, the back of the cereal packet. Read whatever interests you; try to read a little every day. You will begin to notice when something is well-written, and that critical sense will pass into your own writing.

Writing

CHECKLIST 6

- ACCURATE BRIEF AND CLEAR
- Be governed by purpose and reader
- Avoid old-fashioned, hackneyed language
- Use jargon sparingly

- Exterminate clichés
- Cut out tautology
- Beware of empty or loaded words
- Concrete rather than abstract words
- No sentence over 25 words long
- Short introductory paragraph
- Action point in its own paragraph
- Tone: positive, definite, sincere
- Replace passive verbs with active ones

Different Types of Letters

Whatever type of letter we are writing, we must remember two vital elements:

■ The objective of the letter

Why is it being written? What do we want to happen?

■ The relationship with the reader

To whom are we writing? What have they already written to us? What are they expecting from us? How do they feel?

The structure of the letter and its tone will be dictated by these two considerations.

Remember, too, the three cardinal rules of letter writing:

BE POSITIVE: BE DEFINITE: BE SINCERE

■ **Be positive**

Always try to show yourself, and your organization, at their best.

We are out of stock. (Negative)
Stock will be available from 6 October. (Positive)

This model is no longer available. (Negative)
The model you asked for has now been superseded. (Positive)

■ **Be definite**

Vague statements are no good. Promise only what you can deliver.

We will do our best. (Woolly)
We will do this by ... (Specific)
Every effort has been made ... (Waffle)
We have ... (Definite)

■ **Be sincere**

We all hate receiving letters which upset us or make us angry. An emotive response, however, will probably compound the problem rather than solve it. The essence of professional letter writing is to communicate, not with emotion, but with a clear objective.

This does not mean capitulating entirely to the other person's point of view. We should be assertive, acknowledging the problem but making our own position clear.

Your failure to settle this account ... (Angry)
If you have a problem settling this account ... (Helpful)
You evidently have no wish to help. (Accusatory)
I understand that involvement may be difficult. (Assertive)

All your letters are offensive, but this is the last straw. (Emotional)
Perhaps we should meet and discuss the matter. (Cool)

Selling

A sales letter is the ultimate exercise in persuasion. Its purpose is to gain interest, create a belief in the product or service you are selling, and induce the reader to buy.

- Write to those with the authority to buy. Use their name – it attracts a greater response. Form a mental picture of them and their needs. Build the letter around them. The most important selling word of all is *You.*
- Attract attention with a striking introduction: a question, a challenging statement, or an anecdote.
- Arouse interest by appealing to some buying motive (health, personal appearance, image, economy, fear, future prospects).
- Create desire by describing benefits rather than features. A car may include electrically heated seats as a feature: convenience and comfort are the benefits they offer. A computer has innumerable features; your readers want to know only what is of benefit to them.

- Emphasize what is unique about your product: anything topical or new.
- Carry conviction by supporting your sales pitch with guarantees, evidence of testing, after sales service. Clear information, easy to read, and above all concise.
- Use positive words:

need	*security*	*best*
exceptional	*benefits*	*discount*
value	*guaranteed*	*new*
offer	*want*	*special*
exclusive	*unique*	*only*
free	*improved*	*essential*

Avoid 'hype':

fantastic	*fabulous*	*totally extraordinary*

- Induce action by making the letter easy to answer. Set out clear actions and deadlines: make it clear what the reader must do next.
- Provide an incentive to encourage an early reply: a prepaid envelope, a simple form, a free gift.
- Look forward to their reply.

SALES LETTER

BREEDON PARK, Breedon, Berkshire RG99 9XX
Tel: 0111 798593

5 March 1994

Mr B Deasley
Training International
Plenary House
St James's Square
LONDON
W1 6NN

Dear Mr Deasley

As a leading training organization, you need the best available conference facilities at a realistic price.

Breedon Park is the venue you have been looking for.

We are an established country hotel with proven experience in conference management.

We are able to accommodate and cater for 450 guests, and provide excellent technical expertise for every aspect of the event, all at rates which compare exceptionally well with venues of a similar quality.

The hotel is set in 14 acres of parkland, combining the peace and seclusion of the Berkshire woodlands with easy access to both the M4 and Heathrow Airport.

We provide all the services of an exclusive hotel, including two restaurants, cinema, casino, swimming pool, sauna, steam room, whirlpool bath and exercise hall.

Such elements combine to provide the ideal environment for effective management training.

We are happy to enclose our free brochure which lists the organizations which have already benefited from the facilities which we offer. It can only give you a taste here of the facilities Breedon Park offers. To learn more, contact me on the above number to arrange a visit.

Yours sincerely

ALEC FORSYTHE
Sales Manager

Making an enquiry

Any enquiry should be extremely concise and absolutely precise. Ask for exactly what you want: no more and no less.

■ Introduce yourself: perhaps with any specific detail that helps the reader understand why you are enquiring.
■ Say clearly what you want to know.
■ Say why you are asking: *briefly.*
■ Give a clear method of response. Include a telephone number, and any deadline or time limits ('Office hours only').
■ Thank the reader for his or her time and consideration.

ENQUIRY LETTER

'Mon Rêve'
33 Acacia Vista
HOTLEY
Hants
SN45 9BV

14 January 1993

Slick Central Heating Ltd
45 Capstan Street
HOTLEY
Hants
SN45 7HG

Dear Sir or Madam

I am considering converting my central heating system from solid fuel to oil. I would be grateful for any information you can give me in answer to the following questions:

1. The cost, including fitting, of a boiler to replace a Bronco DXC 2 solid fuel boiler. I would also want automatic clock control.
2. An oil storage tank would need to be installed in an external location. Please give an estimate of the cost of such an installation.
3. The present system comprises seven radiators and a heated towel rail. I enclose last year's set of quarterly bills, and would welcome an estimate of running costs under a new system.

4. What arrangements do you make for after-sales servicing, and on what terms?

My wife and I are out working during the day, and so would welcome a letter detailing these aspects of our proposed conversion for consideration at our leisure.

I look forward to your reply.

Yours faithfully

Mr E B Grimthorpe

Answering an enquiry

Answer enquiries promptly – even if it means sending a card acknowledging receipt before the full reply is drafted.

An enquirer is halfway to being a customer. A letter answering an enquiry is halfway to being a sales letter.

- Thank the reader for their enquiry. Welcome it (without making it sound like the first you've received this year!).
- Mention any enclosure in the first paragraph.
- Answer the enquiry *specifically*. Reader's needs before anything else.
- If the incoming letter contains a number of questions, try to answer them in order. If they are tabulated or numbered, number your reply in exactly the same way.
- Add any details which amplify what you know but the reader does not: range of goods, high quality, competitive prices, swift delivery. Keep them relevant.
- Offer carefully any other products or services which have no relation to the original enquiry. The information will be welcome if it is offered but not forced.
- Signal any appropriate action, without committing the customer in advance: a visit from a representative, the address of a local dealer. Contact name and number to make further communication as simple as possible.

LETTER ANSWERING AN ENQUIRY

SLICK CENTRAL HEATING LTD
45 Capstan St., HOTLEY SN45 7HG

Mr E B Grimthorpe
'Mon Rêve'
33 Acacia Vista
HOTLEY
Hants
SN45 9BV

Dear Mr Grimthorpe

Thank you very much for your recent enquiry concerning your central heating system.

Your plan to convert to oil is certainly a wise one. For efficiency and convenience, oil is unrivalled. I enclose a copy of our new brochure, **Oil – the fuel of the future.**

In reply to your questions, in order:

1. The cost of conversion from your present boiler to an oil-fired appliance will vary depending on the boiler chosen. I enclose an example quotation of a boiler equivalent in size to your present solid fuel equipment, including the installation of automatic clock operation as you request.

2. The cost of tank installation is relatively low, and is also included on my example quotation. A little heavy building work may be required to lay a base for the tank.

3. Oil is extremely economical. Assuming your system to be in operation 12 hours a day, and depending on the setting of

the thermostatic control, you can certainly expect a reduction of about 20% (at current rates) on running costs compared to solid fuel.

4. All installation work is guaranteed for twelve months, and the equipment for five years, during which period all servicing of the system is carried out free of charge. Thereafter, we offer a service and insurance plan at an annual cost of £30.

I hope this answers your questions satisfactorily. If you would like to discuss the matter further, please call me on the above number to arrange a visit to your home at a time convenient to you.

Yours sincerely

James Adair
MANAGER

Registering a complaint

Avoid all emotional language: don't blame or whinge! Have all your evidence well researched. If you have been fobbed off before, consider *who* your reader will be: telephone to make certain it's the right person. The reader must be sufficiently senior to be able to take the action you require.

- Introduce yourself
- State what happened. Give evidence.
- Is there any other past history? A receptionist or minor official who gave no satisfaction?
- Say how you feel about the situation, emphasizing actual consequences. Avoid assuming, blaming, or emotive statements.
- Say what you would like to be done, specifically. Give a deadline.

LETTER OF COMPLAINT

6 November 1994

The Manager
Go Fast Car Hire
2 Speeding Lane
LONDON
W1C 3QQ

Dear Sir or Madam

Last Monday morning I hired a car from your West End branch for a business journey to Glasgow.

It became increasingly clear that the condition of the car was completely unsatisfactory.

1. The wheels were unbalanced and the car shook at speeds over 50 mph. I arrived over two hours late and very nearly lost an important deal.
2. On my return trip that evening, I found that the headlamps were out of alignment, so that I was continually flashed by cars travelling in the opposite direction.

Such a car would not have passed an MOT test; yet it was hired out as new with only 1200 miles on the clock. When I returned it on Tuesday morning the receptionist told me, in a very offhand manner, that it was no concern of hers and that I should speak to somebody in the mechanical department. When I went down into the garage, their office was empty.

This is the first time I have used your company. I am not impressed. I have no intention of wasting my valuable time attempting to contact your personnel. I enclose an invoice for the hire, which I have no intention of paying, and would welcome some form of compensation for the inconvenience caused.

Yours faithfully

Jack Lee

Answering a complaint

There are three kinds:

1. Justified: we are in the wrong and must admit it.
2. Unjustified but we will do something to make the reader happy.
3. Unjustified and we are not prepared to help.

It is crucial to choose which response to make. Do not pass the buck: accept responsibility for the response, even if not for the action to be taken. It is not necessarily the complainant's fault that they have written to the wrong person or the wrong department in the organization. To them, *you* are the organization.

Reply type 1: justified

- Thank you for the letter.
- Apologize immediately, and simply. Do not grovel or begrudge.
- Promise that investigation has happened or will happen.
- Action you will take: now: for this particular customer. When. *Do it.*
- Thank the reader: "the complaint has helped us with quality control."

REPLY TO A COMPLAINT 1: JUSTIFIED

TRENDSETTERS

Fly House, Greeb Street, HAVANT HV5 7HH

18 July 1993

Mr G Ripper
38 Leafy Close
CRANKSBURY
Oxfordshire
OX90 4FG

Dear Mr Ripper

Men's trousers: receipt no. 48952

Thank you for your letter and the enclosed garment.

I am very sorry that the trousers should have split in this way, particularly in such embarrassing circumstances. They are certainly designed to be hard-wearing, even on such a hot day as you describe.

I have examined the garment and found that there is indeed a fault in the seam stitching. I have sent it to our quality control department and they are conducting an investigation as a matter of urgency.

I am happy to enclose a gift token to the value of £40, to cover all your costs.

Thank you for taking the trouble to write to us. Your letter has made a positive contribution to our system of quality control. Once again, I apologise for the inconvenience you have been caused, and hope that it will not prevent you from using our stores again in the future.

Yours sincerely

Tunde Oyeleye
QUALITY CONTROL MANAGER

Reply type 2: unjustified but willing to help

- Thank the reader.
- Show immediate sympathy, concern, and understanding (however hard it may be to understand!)
- "Have investigated ..." Make it clear that the problem is not your responsibility: and, gently, that it is the reader's.
- Suggest action the reader might take to stop the problems being repeated. Emphasize points of safety or procedure.
- State the action you are prepared to take. Be positive while not seeming to admit responsibility.
- Thank the reader again.

REPLY TO A COMPLAINT 2:
UNJUSTIFIED BUT WILLING TO HELP

ANIMAL INSPIRATIONS
Hamster House, Unit 1, Rodent Industrial Estate
BASILDON B81 4FG

4 October 1993

Mrs C Hanway
6 Widdicombe Street
SMOKINGHAM
Lancashire
MA44 5VC

Dear Mrs Hanway

Furry Hedgehog Family

Thank you for your letter and the enclosed set of toys.

I was concerned to read of the damage caused by your son, and understand the annoyance and frustration you must feel.

We have inspected the toys carefully and considered the information in your letter. The 'CE' mark on our soft toys covers only reasonable wear and tear, and certainly not total immersion in bleach such as you describe.

Having retrieved the hedgehogs from the lavatory bowl, you should not have boiled them, but soaked them in a mild solution of detergent for a few days. The labels on the toys specify that they should not be washed in temperatures above 30°.

In these exceptional circumstances, we are happy to send a replacement set of furry hedgehogs and hope that they give you, and your son, many years of enjoyment.

Yours sincerely

Vee Harborne
CUSTOMER LIAISON MANAGER

Reply type 3: unjustified and unwilling to help

- Thank the reader.
- Show sympathy, concern, understanding for their point of view.
- "However, our point of view is clearly ..."
- "Because this is our point of view, we cannot help."
- Gently suggest action to prevent repetition of reader's problem.

REPLY TO A COMPLAINT 3:
UNJUSTIFIED AND UNWILLING TO HELP

BRIGHTACRES HOSPITAL TRUST
Jesmond, NEWCASTLE-UPON-TYNE, NE12 8FD

8 February 1993

Miss V Perkins
Flat 5
The Willows
Elm Crescent
SAILINGFORD
Northumbria
NE5 7JK

Dear Miss Perkins

Thank you for your letter of 5 December. We are sorry to hear of your accident in our grounds, especially as you are such a hard-working friend of the hospital.

We have thoroughly investigated the incident, and find that we have no record of any accident at the time you mention. Our security staff man the reception area 24 hours a day, and any accidents are recorded in our accident book.

All steps and paths are gritted in snowy weather, and kept completely free of ice. While therefore appreciating the difficulties you must have been caused, we cannot accept any responsibility for the accident you describe.

We do suggest that, if in future you have an accident in our grounds, you report it immediately and seek medical attention. We will be happy to help.

Thank you again for writing. I hope that you are soon fully recovered and able to take up your visiting duties again.

Yours sincerely

Marie Etienne
SAFETY OFFICER

Getting action

Let down? Fobbed off? Debts unpaid? Goods undelivered? Something needs to be done.

Avoid subjective language. The objective of the letter is to get action, not to antagonize the reader. Be realistic with your demands: what do you expect to achieve? What compromise would you accept?

To whom do you write? Generally, the person who will act: perhaps that person's superior. Going straight to the top may be counterproductive as a first move.

State your facts: supply evidence: dates, names and times. Show that you are reasonable. Be firm but not aggressive.

- Introduce yourself in an initial letter: name and job title.
- Say why you are writing.
- State the facts. Give the evidence. Make sure your information is relevant to the action you require: a threatened breach of contract, an agreement confirmed in writing.
- Emphasize the benefits of prompt action to the reader.
- Say how your organization can help.
- Isolate the action required in a separate paragraph. Be specific: precisely what must be done, by whom, and when.
- Look forward positively to their response.

LETTER GETTING ACTION

HBG IMPORTS LTD
Stapler House, Cedar Road, PORTSMOUTH PO48 1LD

14 May 1994

Mr D Crow
Managing Director
D Crow and Sons
12 Field Walk
LONDON SE13 7HH

Dear Mr Crow

CONTRACT NO 27543/du/5222

As you are aware, your company is constructing a new warehouse at Uxbridge which is due for completion on 1 July 1992.

Earlier this week I became aware of delays. I have on several occasions spoken to your site manager, but unfortunately he has been unable to assure me that the work is progressing satisfactorily.

We are expecting a large consignment of stationery on 8 July, which we are planning to store in the new warehouse. I am concerned that the contract will not be completed on time.

I would draw to your attention clause 5 of our contract which details the compensation due to us in the event of non-completion.

If there are genuine problems, we are willing to give you any help we can to complete the construction.

Please look into this matter urgently, and contact me on the above number to clarify the situation.

Yours sincerely

Peter Blair
LOGISTICS MANAGER

Standard or mailshot letters

Because mailshots are now very easily produced, readers have become more and more sophisticated in recognizing them. Great care must be taken to make them individual.

If you are using the same text over a period of time – or if you are building standard letters from set paragraphs programmed into the word processor – review the text regularly. It is surprising how quickly language seems to date. Take even more care than usual to make the style of the letter personal to you.

- Decide the letter's objective. It must be simple to cover a large number of readers.
- Target the market: build the letter around the *needs* of each reader.
- If there are significant variations between readers, divide the group and adapt the letter for each sub-group.
- Address each reader *by name*. If this means spending an afternoon gathering names on the telephone, so be it. "Dear Managing Director", "Dear Sales Director", "Dear Head Teacher", will guarantee that the letter is destroyed before being read.
- Get your main message across immediately: *before* the reader catches on that the letter is unsolicited and throws it away.
- Keep the information as simple as possible. It is then less likely to be irrelevant.
- Make the tone as personal as you can: say *you* rather than *our customers, our readers,* or *everyone.*
- Use layout to emphasize the message. Anything highlighted by a different colour or typeface, or illustrated in some way, will be noticed first – wherever it is on the page. Remember, though, that the letter is supposed to *look* like a letter: not a brochure.

- Keep the action simple: a telephone number, a pre-paid card.
- Print the letters on adequate equipment. A letter that looks like a computer printout, or uses a different typeface for the reader's name, is counterproductive.
- Sign each letter individually: name and job title. A rubber stamp is as discourteous as it is unnecessary.
- Seal the envelope. A sealed envelope arouses curiosity and makes the letter look less like junk mail.

MAILSHOT LETTER

SLICK CENTRAL HEATING LTD
45 Capstan St., HOTLEY, SN45 7HG

3 June 1994

Mr & Mrs Steiner
74 Inkerman Avenue
HECKRINGTON
Derbyshire
DE88 4MW

Dear Mr & Mrs Steiner

Fashions come and go, but one thing that will never go out of fashion is keeping warm in winter. After all, keeping warm is no more than common sense – especially in our later years.

You may have electric fires, of course, or coal fires, but they are costly and inconvenient. Think of the comfort you could enjoy living in a house that is warm all over – the whole year round.

Can you think of a better gift to yourselves? Or an investment that will add greater value to your home?

Tests have proved that the most cost-efficient, convenient and effective central heating system is fired by oil. Equipped with one of our new, state-of-the-art "Blastomatic" boilers, your home will be heated as well – and as cheaply – as by any other thermostatically-controlled system on the market. The enclosed brochure, **Oil – the fuel of the future,** will convince you of the reasons why.

Some of your friends and neighbours are sure to be using the "Blastomatic" system already. Many thousands of householders have already been convinced of its excellence.

Fill in the enclosed prepaid reply card and we will arrange for Hazel Lovelace, our representative in your area, to call to give further details. She will also be able to give you an estimate of the installation costs. You are under no obligation. Just post the card and leave the rest to us.

And look forward to a future of continuous, luxurious warmth – at the touch of a button.

Yours sincerely

James Adair
MANAGER

Applying for a job

Remember: the purpose of your application is to get an interview, not the job. Everything you send at this stage – the covering letter, the application form and the CV – must make the prospective employer want to see *you*. It must also show that you can follow instructions, organize material, and put your thoughts on paper effectively.

If there is no application form for the post, divide your application into a CV and covering letter. The CV lists past employment, qualifications and perhaps a brief profile of your professional skills. The letter is more personal, giving your reasons for wanting the job, and highlighting why you are suitable to be considered.

The letter, in particular, must be clear, concise and attractive. Always type it unless asked to write by hand.

- Never use your organization's letterhead or address for any job application.
- Always address the reader by name if possible.
- Head the letter with job title and reference number.
- Start and end interestingly. Show enthusiasm.
- Give a summary of your reasons for wanting the job.
- Do not be negative about your present job. Show how what you are doing now is relevant to your application, and how the vacant post differs positively from your present one.
- Emphasize why they should interview *you* rather than anybody else. Highlight one or two of your strongest points: qualifications, skills or experience. Say why you think you are right for the job: briefly and firmly.
- Do not repeat any information given on the application form or CV.

- Ask no questions. Matters of salary, benefits, company car or holidays can be discussed at the interview.
- If writing by hand, print your name in block capitals beneath your signature. Omit your job title.

If you are asked to write a 'supporting statement' on an application form, follow these guidelines:

- Never leave it blank!
- The objective is to give a picture of *you*: your competence at handling material, your knowledge of yourself, your suitability for the job.
- Try to follow any instructions, however vague they may be: "You should use this space to describe any other information which you feel are relevant to your application".
- If no instructions are given, aim at a brief autobiography.
- Write in continuous prose.
- Do not repeat material given in the CV, application form, or covering letter.
- Suggest the reasons why your career has taken the course it has. Emphasize influences on you, your interests, your ideas, ambitions for the future, and above all your *achievements.*
- Draft the statement; edit; re-edit. Do not write on the form until you are certain it is right.
- Fill the space but no more, even if the form invites you to use an extra page.
- If the section on the form asks for specific information which leaves no room for other information you want to give, add the latter to the covering letter.
- Photocopy all the documents you send. You will then be able to take the copies to the interview.

COVERING LETTER WITH A JOB APPLICATION

3 June 1994

Geraldine Fitzwater
Head of Personnel
Valley Electrics Ltd
Farm Road
GIRTFORTH
Lothian
EH78 4DD

Dear Ms Fitzwater

PA to the Managing Director, ref. 44592

I enclose my application form for this post, together with my CV. I believe that my answers show that I am a suitable applicant.

I am presently personal secretary to the managing director of Flowrite Tubings. I have been in post for three years and my duties are listed on my CV.

I read modern languages at Bristol University, and have spent two years working in France and Italy. I would particularly welcome the opportunity to exercise my language skills which the advertised post offers.

At Flowrite, and in my previous jobs, I have developed my secretarial skills and attended a number of training courses. I feel I am ready to extend these skills in a challenging environment, possibly with a view to taking on a more managerial role in the future. I believe that the post advertised would be a logical step in this direction.

I very much hope you feel able to grant me an interview, when I can explain my qualifications and experience more fully.

Yours sincerely

Bena Patel

Checking

Every letter should be checked before it leaves the desk.

Before it slips into its envelope and wings its way to the reader, take a long hard look at it.

- Does it look good? Does it give a good impression of us and our organization? If we were presented with this piece of paper first thing in the morning, would we want to read it?
- Does it achieve its objective?
- Are the reader's needs and expectations met adequately?
- Is the action point clear?
- Is the information accurate? Is it relevant to the purpose and to the needs of the reader? Is it logically set out?
- Does the letter have a heading which is specific but brief?
- Are the paragraphs of manageable length? Are the introduction, and the closing remarks, contained in short paragraphs? Does the first sentence of each paragraph act as a topic sentence for the paragraph as a whole?

... to say how much I appreciated your letter...

- Are there any sentences of 25 words or more? Are the shortest sentences in prominent positions, and the most important words placed most strongly – near the beginning or the end of the sentence?
- Are the words accurate, brief and clear? Are there any which can be replaced with something simpler? Are there any which add nothing and can be removed?
- Are the salutation and complimentary close correct?
- Are all relevant enclosures included?
- Are copies ready to send to anyone who needs them?
- Are spelling, grammar and punctuation correct?

Obviously mistakes in grammar and spelling will not give a good impression. Yet, in truth, these can be the trickiest matters to check.

Every writer should have access to

- A good dictionary
- A thesaurus
- A guide to English usage, examples of which are found in the bibliography.

Grammar

Grammar is a set of rules. You cannot drive without knowing the rules of the road; you should not write without some knowledge of the rules of language.

- Become acquainted with some basic rules of grammar. The most important rules are the simplest ones. Learn to recognize nouns and verbs, adjectives and adverbs. Take it all a bit at a time.
- Write as you would speak.
- Express yourself as simply as possible. Write what you mean, not what you think looks good. You are more likely to be grammatically correct.
- Use your instinct. Read what you have written, *aloud.* If it sounds wrong, it may be wrong.
- Try to isolate any problem, and rephrase in a way that is obviously correct.
- If in doubt, look the matter up in a guide to grammar or usage.
- Note down persistent problems and check your notes regularly.

Spelling

Spelling matters. Whether we like it or not, the way we spell contributes to our public image. However well thought out or elegantly expressed, a letter with spelling errors will inevitably reflect badly on its writer.

Take heart. Everybody has some difficulties with spelling. English is notoriously illogical and inconsistent, and spelling correctly is not made easier at a time when people are reading less than in the past.

■ Think before you write. Clear thoughts make for clear writing.

■ Do not use any word you cannot define precisely. You are more likely to spell correctly words you know well.

■ *Always* use the simpler word rather than the longer, complicated one.

■ If in doubt: write the word quickly. Does it look right? First guesses are often correct. However:

■ *Never* rely on guessing. Check with a dictionary.

■ Use a *good* dictionary: one that is too big to fit comfortably in a bag! A pocket dictionary for the handbag or briefcase is useful for emergencies.

■ Do not rely on the dictionary on your WP: it will not be comprehensive, and may include American spellings.

■ Keep a notebook for words that refuse to stick in your mind. Note down any misspellings or unfamiliar words you come across, and take a few minutes every day to check yourself against the list.

■ Do not rely on spellcheckers: they will not recognize the difference between *their* and *there,* between *place* and *plaice,* or between *cannot* and *can not.*

■ Use a thesaurus to improve your vocabulary and clarify meaning.

Try to leave a little time after writing before you check the letter. Always be ready to ask a friend or colleague for comments.

Writing well is a matter of practice; it cannot be learnt overnight. Once you have begun to follow the practical guidelines in this book, you will enjoy the real pleasure of having language at your command.

If, on inspection, your letter passes all the stages of your checklist, you can be sure that it will do its job well. It will be an excellent ambassador for the organization, and a credit to you: the hard-working, caring, fastidious writer of that most important document – the business letter.

Checking

CHECKLIST 8

- CLEAR: CONCISE: COMPLETE: CORRECT
- Does the letter look good: layout, typeface, margins?
- Does it achieve its objectives?
- Are the reader's needs met fully?
- Are names and addresses correct?
- Does the letter have a clear heading?
- Is the information accurate, and logically ordered?
- Is the style consistent and friendly?
- Is the action highlighted; what/by whom/when?
- Salutation and close correct?
- All enclosures included?
- Spelling, grammar and punctuation OK?
- Copies to all who need them?
- Does it give a good impression: us; the organization?

Appendix A

A checklist for dictation

Preparation

- Prepare yourself. Clear you mind, desk – and mouth!
- Prepare the material: a clear outline on paper.
- Prepare your priorities: important letters first.
- Prepare the typist: give all relevant papers. Supply all the relevant information:
  - the reader's name;
  - the writer's name;
  - the reference;
  - how many copies are needed;
  - to whom the copies are to be sent;
  - any relevant incoming letter; if so, which one.

Dictating

- Find a quiet place, free from interruptions.
- Say it simply: short sentences; one idea per paragraph.
- Punctuate clearly. Pause in reading to help meaning.
- Speak slowly and clearly.
- Spell unfamiliar names and technical terms.
- When dictating into a machine:
  - allow time for the machine to switch on;
  - do not dictate in the car or train;
  - check that the machine is working – every time;
  - include all instructions, before dictating;
  - if you stop, stop the machine. Collect your thoughts; rewind; play back; set to record and continue.
  - check when you have finished. *Remember to switch off!*

Appendix B

Forms of address and salutation

Title	Envelope	Salutation
Duke	His Grace the Duke of ...	My Lord Duke; Your Grace
Duchess	Her Grace the Duchess of ...	Madam
Earl	The Rt Hon the Earl of ...	My Lord
Countess	The Rt Hon the Countess of ...	Madam
Viscount	The Rt Hon the (Lord) Viscount	My Lord
Baron	The Rt Hon Lord	My Lord
Knight	Sir John Black	Sir; Dear Sir John
Knight's wife	Lady Black	Madam
Archbishop	His Grace the Lord A of ...	My Lord A.

Bishop	The Rt Rev the Lord B of ...;	My Lord B.
		Lord B of ...;
	The Lord B of	
Clergy	The Reverend Robert	Dear Mr Brown
	Brown (DD)	(Dear Dr B)
Privy	The Rt Hon Michael Jones MP	Dear Sir
Councillor		
MP	Kevin Johnson MP	Dear Sir
Doctor	Dr Geraldine Smith	Dear Dr Smith

Qualifications after the name

In this order:

1. decorations (military; civil);
2. degrees and diplomas;
3. membership of professional bodies.

Reference: *Titles and Forms of Address*, publ. A & C Black.

Appendix C

Writing Numbers

The general rule

■ Write numbers from one to ten as words; as figures from 10 up.

Most chairs have four legs.
The book contained 134 pages.

Exceptions

■ Numbers as words at the beginning of a sentence:

Fourteen students passed their exams this term.

Try not to start a sentence with a huge or complicated number!

■ Round numbers spelled out as words:

Some two hundred employees were made redundant.

■ Adjoining numbers: spell out the smaller or the first number:

five 10p pieces;
three 50ml teaspoons

■ Quantities and measurements as figures:

23 July; Fig.5; 45 Nunhead Grove; 2%

■ Ordinal numbers in words, unless in a list:

the first man on the moon;
1st prize; 2nd prize; 3rd prize

■ Sums of money as figures;

£467.21; $50; 25p

■ Numbers in parallel constructions as figures:

He bought 3 books, 23 pens,
7 pencils and 6 packets of paper.

 # Bibliography

Dictionaries

Chambers English Dictionary, Chambers, 1990
Chambers Concise Dictionary, new edition, Chambers, 1991

The Shorter Oxford English Dictionary, 2 vols., Oxford, 1973
The Concise Oxford Dictionary, 8th ed., Oxford, 1990
The Pocket Oxford Dictionary, 8th ed., Oxford, 1992

Pay your money and take your choice. **The Shorter Oxford English Dictionary** is probably the best affordable dictionary on the market, but its bulk makes it more suitable for the home than for the office.

Roget's Thesaurus, ed. B. Kirkpatrick, Penguin, 1988

The classic 'vocabulary on a large scale, categorized by topics'. Invaluable for discovering new words or recovering forgotten ones.

Guides to grammar and usage

Fowler, H. W., **A Dictionary of Modern English Usage**, 2nd ed. rev. Sir Ernest Gowers, Oxford, 1965

The most famous guide to English usage. Indispensable, if rather puritanical.

Gowers, Sir Ernest, **The Complete Plain Words**, Penguin, 1986

Originally commissioned by the Treasury in 1948, this book has had a profound impact on language use in the Civil Service and beyond. Repeatedly re-printed and often revised, the latest edition includes a useful checklist of words and phrases to be used with care.

Greenbaum, Sidney, **An Introduction to English Grammar**, Longman, 1991

A comprehensive, thoroughly modern survey. Very academic: not for the faint-hearted.

Partridge, Eric, **Usage and Abusage**, Penguin, 1973

A useful companion to Fowler, Partridge is entertaining and full of good sense.

Phythian, B. A., **Teach Yourself English Grammar**, Hodder & Stoughton, 1984

– **Teach Yourself Correct English**, Hodder & Stoughton, 1985

Straightforward, approachable guides to grammar and usage, including plenty of exercises and sections on applied writing: reports, letters and so on.

Other books of interest

Buzan, Tony, **Use Your Head,** rev. ed., BBC, 1989

The definitive guide to pattern plans – or, as Buzan calls them, Mind Maps.

Gartside, L., **Modern Business Correspondence,** 4th ed., Pitman, 1986

As comprehensive a guide to writing letters as you could wish. Resolutely old-fashioned, however, and littered with spelling mistakes. To be used with care.

Jones, Alan, **How to Write a Winning C.V.,** Hutchinson, 1990

Full of tips on making job applications.

Stanton, Nicki, **Communication,** 2nd ed., Macmillan, 1990

An excellent survey of business communications in general, including a useful section on letters.

Titles and Forms of Address, 19th ed., publ. A & C Black, 1990

How to address anyone you could possibly want to address.